The Country Kitchen
PARTY
DISHES
Jean Hatfield

The Country Kitchen

PARTY
DISHES

Jean Hatfield

HARLAXTON
PUBLISHING

*Front and back jacket: A buffet table spread ready for
the hungry party guests. Left to right: rice Tyrolbof (p.
43), oven-fried lemon chicken (p. 30), spinach salad
with yogurt dressing (p. 39), sweet sherry trifle (p.
41), oysters Kilpatrick (p. 17) and galantine of veal
(p. 23).*

*Front and back endpapers: An old-fashioned country
kitchen with the preparation for a spicy fruit cake in
the foreground. The wood - burning stove is wonderful for long, slow cooking.*

*Page 2: Devils on horseback are an old party favorite.
They can be prepared the day before and broiled just
before serving.*

*COOK'S NOTES: Standard spoon measurements
are used in all recipes.
All spoon measurements are level.
All ovens should be preheated to the specified
temperature.*

*Fresh herbs are used unless otherwise stated. If they
are unavailable, use half the quantity of dried herbs.
Use freshly ground black pepper whenever pepper is
used; add salt and pepper to taste. Use all-purpose
flour unless otherwise stated. Fresh ginger root is used
unless otherwise stated. Use fresh chilies or half the
quantity of dried. I use cold-pressed virgin olive oil
but any type may be used. Vinegar is white wine fer-
mented vinegar.*

Published by Harlaxton Publishing Ltd
2 Avenue Road, Grantham, Lincolnshire, NG31 6TA, United Kingdom.
A Member of the Weldon International Group of Companies.

First published in 1992.
Reprinted in 1993.

© Copyright Harlaxton Publishing Ltd
© Copyright design Harlaxton Publishing Ltd

Publishing Manager: Robin Burgess
Project Coordinator: Barbara Beckett
Designer: Barbara Beckett
Illustrator: Amanda McPaul
Photographer: Ray Jarratt
Editor in United Kingdom: Alison Leach
Typeset in United Kingdom: Seller's, Grantham
Produced in Singapore by Imago

British Library Cataloguing-in-Publication data.
A catalogue record for this book is available from the British Library.
Title: Country Kitchen Series: Party Dishes
ISBN:1 85837 009 4

CONTENTS

COOKING FOR PARTIES

WHETHER you are cooking for two people or fifty, preparing for a party should be fun. That is why I have given you delicious recipes with simple straightforward instructions. Throughout the book you will find handy tips on the preparation and storage of food to help make your party a success.

There are recipes in this book to serve from four to twenty people. Many of them may be doubled successfully–just remember that you should use *less* than twice the recommended liquid when you double the other ingredients. On the other hand, if you are halving a recipe, use *more* than half the recommended quantity of liquid specified.

Parties range from intimate dinners for two or four, to cocktail parties, to buffet-style meals for a large crowd. So you will find a variety of recipes here, from finger food to roasts, and from brandy snaps to trifle. Whatever kind of party you organize, the key to success is in the planning. Will the guests be seated while they eat? How will the food be carried and served? Should food be cold or hot? Answers to these practical questions will help you choose a menu that suits the place as well as the occasion.

Many of the recipes I have given can be prepared ahead. Some served cold, others need to be reheated but whichever you choose, they should be a great success. Remember to read the recipe through and make a complete shopping list. You should also check to see that you have suitable cooking pans and serving dishes to cope with the recipe. Perhaps you could borrow some extra serving platters from a good friend or neighbour, and return the favor on another occasion.

If your party is to be held out-of-doors, it is best to choose dishes that are easy to serve. If you have a distance to travel, you will need to be sure you can keep some dishes cool while you are transporting them–egg custard and mayonnaise, for instance, shouldn't be allowed to warm up.

Above all, don't forget that parties should be happy occasions and that the cook should enjoy the festivities too. You will find great satisfaction in presenting a special festive meal, but make sure you plan well in advance and simplify the work you have to do at the last minute. That way, you will not be too tired or busy to join in the fun. Enjoy your party!

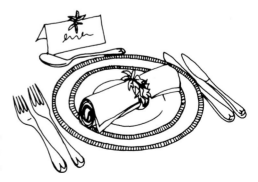

If you are nervous about cooking fish, then this recipe is for you. Trout in white wine is a perfect dish for a dinner party as you can prepare everything well in advance and keep it refrigerated.

STARTERS

WHETHER you call these dishes hors d'oeuvres, starters, appetizers, or entrées, they can be used for many occasions–light lunches, cocktail parties or as a first course for a dinner party. Just remember, however, that starters should whet the appetite, not saturate it, and should harmonize with the main course that follows. When serving food at a cocktail party, be sure to present it attractively and at the correct temperature either chilled or piping hot.

Sandwiches

Dainty sandwiches that can be eaten in two or three bites are my favorite to serve with drinks.

They can be made in advance and you can choose such delicious fillings as thinly cut ham, turkey roll, smoked salmon, and cream cheese with herbs. You can ask your deli to slice the bread thinly or, if that is not possible, firm the loaf in the freezer for an hour and cut it with a proper bread saw or a very sharp knife.

The important point when making sandwiches is to organize the fillings. Whip the butter, have ready foil or waxed paper to wrap the sandwiches and plastic bags or boxes to store them in the refrigerator. Sandwiches will keep in excellent condition for up to 24 hours if wrapped in the following way.

Stack the filled sandwiches in bundles of three, place an outside lettuce leaf on top then cover closely in plastic wrap. When you have made six packages, place them in plastic boxes or bags for preference and store in the refrigerator or a cool room. When ready to serve, trim the crusts and cut into fingers or triangles.

Cucumber Sandwiches

Small, perfect cucumber sandwiches are the ideal accompaniment to iced tea in the yard. Like tomato sandwiches, they are best assembled just before serving, but you can have the butter whipped, the cucumber sliced and salted, and the lettuce crisping in the refrigerator in advance. To prepare the cucumber, peel and slice it thinly, place on a flat plate, sprinkle with a teaspoon of salt, and leave to stand for 30 minutes. Drain and sprinkle with a few drops of vinegar. Place between thin slices of buttered white bread with finely shredded lettuce and season with pepper. Trim and cut with a good, sharp, serrated bread knife, and serve.

Asparagus Boats

Boat-shaped molds are available at kitchen supply stores and they look most attractive. I have given the recipe for cheese pastry but you can use ready-rolled short crust pastry if you wish.

FOR THE CHEESE DOUGH
1/2	cup butter
1 1/2	cips flour
2	cups rattrap cheese,grated
	A pinch of salt
	A dash of cayenne
2	tablespoons cold water

FOR THE FILLING
2	tablespoons butter
3	slices streaky bacon, diced
3	scallions, chopped
1	cup light cream
3	tablespoons grated parmesan cheese
3	eggs, beaten

Salt and pepper
1 1/2 pounds canned asparagus tips

Cucumber sandwiches being made ready to serve at a summer tea party.

Cream the butter and mix well with the other dough ingredients. Form into a ball, cover in plastic wrap and leave it in the refrigerator for at least 1 hour.

Roll out the dough thinly on a lightly floured board. Grease 12 molds with butter. Arrange close together. Lift the sheet of dough on a rolling pin and place loosely over the molds. Roll a small piece of dough into a ball and dip in flour. Use this to press the dough into the mold, then roll a well-floured rolling pin over the top (one way, then the other) to remove surplus dough. Roll out the trimmings again and use to line the remaining molds.

Melt the butter and fry the bacon and scallions until the bacon is beginning to crisp. Add the cream and heat only until bubbles form; do not allow to boil. Remove from the heat, stir in the cheese, then the eggs, and season with salt and pepper.

Drain the asparagus and place a few tips in each dough shell.

Arrange the molds on a baking sheet and carefully pour in the filling to come almost to the top of the molds. Bake in a preheated moderate oven (350°F) for 15-20 minutes, or until the filling is puffed and golden and a knife inserted in the center comes out clean. Serve warm or cold on the hors d'oeuvre tray.
Makes 12-14.

Minted Citrus Cocktail

This makes a nice contrast to a rich meal and is a favorite starter for Christmas dinner.

5   cups grapefruit segments
1   cup canned mandarin segments
1/2   cup orange juice
1/2   teaspoon Angostura bitters
1   tablespoon sherry
      Sprigs of mint
8   maraschino cherries

Drain the grapefruit and mandarin segments and turn into a large bowl or jar. Add the orange juice, bitters and sherry and mix gently. Chill overnight.

Spoon the fruit cocktail into small, iced glass dishes. Decorate with mint sprigs and maraschino cherries. Serves 8.

Devils on Horseback

Prepare these well in advance and cook just before serving.

20   large prunes, pitted
20   whole blanched almonds
7   slices bacon

Stuff the prunes with the almonds. Stretch the bacon with the back of a knife, then cut each slice in three. Wrap each prune in a piece of bacon and secure with a wooden toothpick. Broil for 4-5 minutes on each side, until the bacon is crisp, or cook on crumpled paper towel in a microwave oven for 3-4 minutes. Makes 20.

Cocktail Meatballs

These meatballs are delicious served on toothpicks and can be made in advance, packed into plastic containers and frozen. Serve these with a piquant dip.

2   pounds lean ground beef
1   pound sausage meat
2   large potatoes
1   medium-sized Granny Smith apple
2   large onions
2   slices bacon
2   eggs
2   teaspoons curry powder
1   teaspoon ground ginger
2   teaspoons superfine sugar
1/4   teaspoon dry mustard
      Salt and pepper
1   tablespoon tomato ketchup
      Flour for coating
      Oil for frying

Peel and dice potatoes and apple. Finely chop onion. Place in a saucepan and just cover with water. Bring to a boil, then reduce heat and simmer until tender. Rub through a strainer, then mash and allow to cool.

Chop the bacon finely and lightly beat eggs. Place all ingredients in a bowl and mix well together. Using all-purpose flour, roll into bite-sized balls (place a little flour in a cup, add a small spoonful of mixture and quickly roll into a ball).

Heat a little oil in a skillet and fry the meatballs until golden. Drain on paper towels and serve hot or cold. The meatballs can also be baked in a moderately hot oven (375°F) for 15-20 minutes or until golden Makes about 100.

COOK'S NOTES: *The best method to prevent bacon slices sticking to the pan is to start cooking the slices on a cold surface and bring the heat up gently.*

Opposite: This recipe makes a large quantity of cocktail meatballs, a tasty offering to serve at the beginning of a party.

Oysters Rockefeller

A superb dish for a special occasion. You can buy packets of frozen chopped spinach from the freezer in supermarkets.

24	oysters on the shell
3/4	cup sour cream
2	garlic cloves, crushed with a little salt
	Pepper
1	cup cooked spinach, finely chopped
6	tablespoons fine white bread crumbs
2	tablespoons grated rattrap cheese
2	tablespoons butter

Remove the oysters from their shells. Mix half the sour cream with half the crushed garlic and season with pepper. Place a teaspoon of the mixture in the bottom of each shell and place the oyster back in the shell.

Combine the spinach with the remaining sour cream and garlic, season with pepper and place a tablespoon of this mixture on each oyster.

Sprinkle with the bread crumbs and cheese. Arrange the oysters on rock salt in an ovenproof dish and place a small piece of butter on each. Place under a preheated broiler for about 4 minutes or until the bread crumbs are a golden brown. Serve hot. Serves 4.

Mushrooms Coriander

Fresh cilantro soup to serve as a starter for a summer lunch or dinner.

The combined flavors of the orange-scented coriander and the bay leaves give a wonderful flavor to this dish. It may be served as a first course in little dishes with crusty bread.

2	pounds small white mushrooms, quartered or whole
1/3	cup lemon juice
4	teaspoons coriander seeds
1/3	cup olive oil
3	bay leaves
	Salt and pepper

Clean the mushrooms with a cloth dipped in water and lemon juice. Trim the stalks. Cut the mushrooms into quarters and squeeze some lemon juice over them.

Crush the coriander seeds in a mortar or with a rolling pin. Heat the olive oil in a heavy skillet over a low heat. Add the coriander seeds and allow to heat through. Add the mushrooms and bay leaves. Season with salt and pepper. Cook for 1 minute. Cover the skillet and allow the mushrooms to cook for a further 5 minutes over a very low heat, then leave to cool.

Place the mushrooms in a dish and store in the refrigerator until required. Serves 8.

Cilantro Soup

This delicious soup is excellent made with chicken stock and fresh cilantro leaves which are usually obtainable from the supermarket or the herb can be grown in a warm spot in your own garden. In warm weather the plants will mature in six weeks.

1	cup chopped celery
1	cup chopped onion
2	teaspoons grated ginger root
1	garlic clove, crushed
1	tablespoon butter
1	tablespoon olive oil
1	tablespoon flour
1 1/4	quarts chicken stock, heated
1	cup fresh cilantro leaves
	Salt and pepper
1	cup sour cream
	Lemon juice
	A few extra cilantro leaves

Heat butter and oil in a heavy-based saucepan and slowly cook the celery, onion, ginger root and garlic until soft. Sprinkle the softened vegetables with flour, slowly add the heated stock, bring to a boil, then reduce heat and simmer for 10 minutes. Remove from heat and stir in the cilantro leaves. Leave to stand for 10 minutes then purée in the food processor.

If serving hot, reheat, then stir in the sour cream and lemon juice. Garnish each portion with cilantro leaves. If serving chilled, refrigerate overnight and add the sour cream just before serving. Serves 6.

COOK'S NOTES: Bacon keeps best wrapped in waxed paper and foil, then stored in the refrigerator.

Melon & Ham

Be sure to have prosciutto cut into wafer-thin slices and store it tightly wrapped, in the refrigerator. Prepare this starter just before serving.

1	large honeydew melon
3	ounces prosciutto
1	lemon

Slice the melon into crescents and remove seeds, fiber and rind. Wrap each crescent in wafer-thin slices of prosciutto and garnish each serving with half a slice of lemon. Serves 8.

COOK'S NOTES: Before vine leaves can be wrapped around a filling, they need to be blanched, that is dropped into boiling water, then into cold. This makes them pliable and gets rid of insecticides. When picking your own vine leaves, pick the leaves third or fourth from the tip as they are the most tender. Goat's cheese cut into logs, wrapped in vine leaves, then broiled or barbecued, makes a really special first course.

Melon with Port

If you wish, you can scoop out the melon with a teaspoon or melon-baller, mix the flesh with port and return to the melon and, after chilling, serve in glass dishes.

2   small, sweet melons
      superfine sugar (optional)
4-6   tablespoons port

Cut the top off the melon and use a teaspoon to remove seeds and membrane from the center. If the melon is not sweet enough, sprinkle the inside with the sugar. Pour port into the melon, replace the top, wrap in plastic wrap and chill for at least 1 hour. Serves 8.

SEAFOOD

Japanese Salmon Salad

If you are a fan of Japanese food you will love this salad. It is rich and sustaining and the more unusual ingredients are available at specialty stores. Wasabi, the green horseradish powder, is very strong so measure the amount carefully.

1   pound fresh salmon fillets
4   small avocados
3   teaspoons lemon juice
2   teaspoons wasabi
3   tablespoons light soy sauce
      Shredded nori seaweed
      Bean sprouts

Remove skin from the salmon and cut the flesh into small cubes. Halve avocados, remove the stones and peel. Cut into small cubes and toss gently in lemon juice to prevent discoloring.

Blend the wasabi with a little water to make a paste, then mix in the soy sauce. Toast the nori over a flame or under the broiler and use scissors to cut into thin strips. Just before serving, add the soy dressing to the salmon and avocado cubes and toss lightly. Arrange bean sprouts on individual plates and mound the salad on top. Sprinkle salads with the toasted nori strips and bean sprouts. Serves 8.

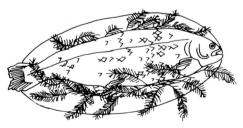

Baked buttered mussels make delicious finger food to hand around at a party. Be sure to serve them with plenty of small paper napkins.

COOKS NOTES: To make horseradish sauce, combine sour cream, lemon juice and horseradish cream. Season with salt, pepper and paprika. Place in a sauce boat and hand around with fish.

Baked Buttered Mussels

1	tablespoon oil
4	dozen mussels, cleaned
1/4	cup butter
1/4	teaspoon garlic salt, (optional)

Rub a large baking dish with oil and arrange mussels in a single layer. Place in very hot oven (450°F) for 5-10 minutes, until the shells open. Do not overcook. Remove upper shells.

Melt butter, add garlic salt. Serve the mussels on the lower shells with a little butter and any liquid that has escaped into the pan poured over. Serves 4.

Cold Salmon Trout

Fresh salmon or sea trout is a great delicacy shown to its best advantage when cooked whole and served cold. It makes a lovely centerpiece for a small wedding reception in the garden, wreathed in feathery fennel leaves.

4	pounds salmon trout, cleaned
	Salt
2	bulbs of fennel, complete with fronds
1	cup dry white wine

Cover your longest baking sheet or dish with a double thickness of foil, just large enough to enclose the fish. Season the salmon trout with a little salt and tuck some fronds of fennel in the opening of the fish. Wash the fennel bulbs and slice finely, sprinkle a layer of fennel on the foil and place the fish on top. Cover with remaining fennel and pour over the wine. Enclose the fish in foil and bake in a preheated oven (375°F) for 25-30 minutes. The old rule is usually to allow 10 minutes for each 1-inch thickness of the fish at it's thickest point. Take care not to over cook, and remember the fish will continue to cook a little as it cools. Remove from the oven and leave until cool enough to handle.

Unwrap the fish, transfer it to a large serving dish and discard the cooked fennel. Make a neat cut through the skin in a curved line behind the head. Gently pull off the skin, leaving the tail intact. Wipe the dish and when cool decorate the trout and the dish with sprigs of fresh fennel. Serve with mayonnaise.
Serves 10-12.

Oysters Kilpatrick are delicious because the oysters retain their essential flavor. Chop the bacon as finely as possible for the best result.

Oysters Kilpatrick

Oyster lovers argue as to the best way to serve them. While no one disagrees that fresh oysters are wonderful served simply with a dash of lemon juice or tabasco sauce, *Oysters Kilpatrick* come a close second.

2	dozen oysters on the half shell
2	teaspoons Worcestershire sauce
2	tablespoons butter
2	slices bacon, finely chopped
	Pepper

Arrange the oysters in a broiler. Heat the sauce and butter then spoon over the oysters. Sprinkle each oyster with finely chopped bacon and place under a heated broiler for 3 minutes or until the oysters are plump and the bacon crisp. Season with pepper and serve immediately. Serves 4.

Trout in White Wine

An excellent way of cooking trout which is now so readily available.

8	trout
	Salt and pepper
4	tablespoons chopped herbs
	(parsley, thyme and a little sage)
2	teaspoons grated lemon rind
1	tablespoon butter
1 1/2	cups chablis or other white wine
1	tablespoon each butter : flour, blended
1	tablespoon tomato paste
1	cup light cream

Wash, dry and season the trout. Place the fish in a buttered ovenproof dish. Sprinkle with the chopped herbs and lemon rind. Pour the wine around the fish and dot with knobs of butter. Cover with a piece of waxed paper and cook in a moderate oven (350°F) for 15-20 minutes. Drain the trout and arrange on a warm serving

Salmon mousse is a classic starter for a dinner party. Be careful to discard all the bones and skin when removing the salmon from the can.

dish. Keep hot.

Strain the liquor from the fish into a small pan. Whisk in the blended butter and flour and tomato paste, pour in the cream and cook for 2-3 minutes, stirring frequently. Coat the fish carefully with this sauce. Serves 8.

Potted Shrimp

Potted shrimp make a very simple but memorable first course. I usually buy frozen shrimp for this treatment as they are the cheapest. Double the quantity for 8 people.

1	*pound peeled shrimp*
3/4	*cup butter*
1/4	*teaspoon ground mace*
1/4	*teaspoon grated nutmeg*
	A pinch of cayenne
1	*teaspoon ground mixed spice*
	Pepper

Cut the shrimp into two or three pieces. Melt the butter in a large skillet and when the foam subsides add the shrimp and the mace, nutmeg, cayenne, mixed spice and pepper. Toss in the butter for a few minutes.

Spoon or pour into four small ramekins or small soufflé dishes. Press lightly, then cover with round pieces of foil and chill in the refrigerator. Serve with Melba toast. Serves 4.

Salmon Mousse

An excellent first course for a dinner party or a delicious summer lunch.

	Half a cucumber
2	*tablespoons French dressing*
3	*teaspoons gelatin*
3	*tablespoons boiling water*
1	*8-ounce can salmon*
1	*tablespoon mayonnaise*
2/3	*cup heavy cream, chilled and whipped*
	Salt and pepper
	A few drops of red food coloring (optional)
	Lettuce, tomato and lemon slices

Dice half of the cucumber and steep in the French dressing. Peel the remaining cucumber and cut into thick slices. Boil for 5 minutes in salted water and drain well. Dissolve the gelatin in the boiling water, stirring thoroughly. Put the salmon, including juice, boiled cucumber, mayonnaise, dissolved gelatin, with salt and pepper into a blender and blend on high speed until smooth. Adjust seasoning and add a few drops of coloring, if liked. Blend again until combined. Add the diced cucumber, and fold in the cream. Wet the mold and pour in the salmon mixture. Chill until set. To serve, turn out onto a dish and garnish with lettuce leaves, tomato and slices of lemon. Serve with horseradish sauce. Serves 4.

Marinated Tuna Fish

4	*fresh tuna cutlets*
	FOR THE MARINADE
	Juice of 1 orange
1/4	*cup soy sauce*
2	*tablespoons chopped parsley*
1	*tablespoon lemon juice*
1	*garlic clove, crushed*
1	*teaspoon garam masala*

Mix the orange juice, soy sauce, parsley, lemon juice, garlic and garam masala. Place tuna cutlets in marinade and allow to stand for 3 hours.

Remove tuna from the marinade and place in a skillet. Baste with the remaining marinade and cook for about 4 minutes per side.

Serve with a green salad tossed in lemon juice. Serves 4.

Rollmop Salad

An excellent winter salad. Rollmops are obtainable at good delicatessens and can be stored in the refrigerator for several days.

6	*rollmops*
2/3	*cup French dressing*
1	*teaspoon superfine sugar*
1/2	*teaspoon dry mustard*
	Salt and pepper
4	*potatoes, boiled*
2	*beets, cooked*
	Crisp lettuce leaves
2	*red apples, cut into cubes*
8	*dill pickles, sliced .*

Cut rollmops into strips. Mix the French dressing with the sugar and mustard. Season to taste with salt and pepper.

Dice the potatoes and beets. Fold them into the dressing. Place lettuce on a flat serving dish, add potato and beets and top with rollmops. Arrange the apple cubes and slices of dill pickle around the side. Serves 8.

MEAT

Stuffed Pork Roast

This is an excellent recipe for those who love pork crust and is a wonderful dish for a dinner party.

2 1/2 pound piece of pork belly
FOR THE STUFFING
8   ounces pork-and-veal mince
8   ounces fresh bread crumbs
1   medium sized onion, finely chopped
1   egg, beaten
1   tablespoon chopped parsley
1/2 teaspoon ground sage,
     oregano or rosemary
     Salt and pepper

Ask the butcher to remove bones and score the rind. Rub skin with a little oil, salt and, if possible, leave to rest overnight in the refrigerator.

With a knife, make a shallow incision down the center of the belly meat, cutting towards but not through to the rind, and make two pockets. Combine the stuffing ingredients and place in the pockets in the meat.

Roll the meat so that the two long ends meet around the stuffing, tie firmly at 1-inch intervals. Give the rind a second rubbing with salt and place on a rack in an open roaster. (This is important if you want every square inch of crust, as the rind will never become crisp at the point of contact with the baking dish.)

Bake in a preheated very hot oven (450°F) for 30 minutes, then reduce to 375°F for a further 1¼ hours. Potatoes may be baked around the meat.

Remove to a warmed serving dish. Pour off excess fat and make gravy. If you like, stir in 1 tablespoon of chunky marmalade. Serves 8.

Sauerbraten

I was given this recipe by a German friend. It is delicious and can be made ahead and reheated just before serving.

3   pounds shin beef
2   cups vinegar or wine
2   cups water
2   onions, sliced
2   bay leaves
2   teaspoons salt
1   teaspoon black peppercorns
1   garlic clove, crushed
1/4 cup soft brown sugar or honey
     Flour
2   tablespoons oil or drippings
2/3 cup sour cream

Cut beef into 1/2-inch slices and place in a heat-proof dish. Prepare a marinade by combining vinegar or wine, water, onions, bay leaves, salt, peppercorns, garlic and sugar or honey. Heat gently but do not allow to boil. Pour the hot marinade over the meat, cover and when cool, store in refrigerator for 4-8 days. Turn meat each day.

When ready to cook, drain the meat and set the marinade aside.

Pat the meat dry and roll in seasoned flour. Brown the meat in oil or dripping, add sliced onions, if desired, and half the marinade. Simmer gently for 1½ hours, adding more marinade if necessary.

Just before serving, season with salt and thicken gravy: combine 2 tablespoons flour with 1/2 cup cold water or marinade, add to the sauerbraten, bring to a boil and cook gently for a few minutes.

Roast stuffed pork looks spectacular and is a surprisingly inexpensive dish to make.

Add the sour cream to the thickened gravy but don't allow the cream to boil. Serve with boiled or mashed potatoes. Serves 8.

COOK'S NOTES: Bread crumbs give a wonderful finish to many dishes and are easily made. Take day-old bread, remove the crusts, then cut into even slices. Bake in a moderate oven till they are dry and golden, allow to cool, and process in a blender. Rub through a strainer and store in an airtight jar. You may like to bake the crusts till crisp, then serve with soups. It is not advisable to mix the crusts with the main part of the bread as your food will look patchy if fried with this combination.

Veal Marengo

A favorite Italian dish very suitable for a small dinner party. Serve with pasta or steamed rice.

1 1/2 *pounds veal shoulder*
2 *tablespoons oil*
2 *medium sized onions, finely chopped*
1 *tablespoon flour*
1 *tablespoon tomato paste*
1/2 *cup white wine*
1 1/2 *cups water or stock*
2 *garlic cloves, crushed with a little salt*
  A bouquet garni
1/2 *pound tomatoes,*
  peeled and roughly chopped
  Pepper
1/4 *pound mushrooms*
  Chopped parsley
  Triangles of fried bread

Cut the meat into 2-inch cubes. Heat oil in a saucepan and brown the meat a few pieces at a time. Remove from the pan, add onions and cook slowly until golden, then dust with flour and continue cooking until brown.

Remove the pan from the heat, stir in tomato paste, wine and 1-cup of stock and blend until smooth. Return to the heat and stir until boiling. Reduce the heat, add meat, garlic, bouquet garni and tomatoes. Season with pepper, cover and simmer 45-60 minutes, stirring occasionally. Add more stock if needed.

Slice the mushrooms thickly. Add to the veal for the last 10 minutes of cooking. Season to taste and garnish with parsley and fried bread. Serves 6.

Galantine of Veal

This elegant Italian dish is best made a few days in advance. Some butchers only sell ground mixed pork-and-veal which you can substitute for the veal and pork in the stuffing.

5	*pounds boneless veal, loin or shoulder*
1	*tablespoon butter*
2	*onions, sliced*
2	*carrots, sliced*
1	*cup beef stock*
1	*cup dry white wine*
1	*bay leaf*
1	*stalk celery*
	Sprig of thyme
	Salt and pepper

FOR THE PORK-AND-VEAL STUFFING

1	*tablespoon butter*
2	*scallions, chopped*
4	*ounces ham steak, diced*
1	*pound ground veal*
1	*pound ground pork*
1	*tablespoon pine nuts*
2	*tablespoons stuffed olives, sliced*
1	*tablespoon chopped parsley*
2	*eggs, lightly beaten*
	Salt and pepper

Opposite: A wonderful addition to the buffet table. I always know I'll make my guests happy when I serve this aromatic galantine of veal.

TO MAKE PORK-AND-VEAL STUFFING

Melt the butter, add the scallions and cook for 2-3 minutes. Place in a large mixing bowl, add all the other ingredients and mix well.

Remove any excess fat and gristle from the veal and lay it out flat. Spread with pork-and-veal stuffing. Form a neat roll and sew up with strong thread or tie with string.

TO PREPARE THE MEAT

Melt the butter in an open roaster and lightly brown the roll on all sides. Remove. Add the onions and carrots and cook for a few minutes. Lay the browned meat on top and pour over stock and wine. Add bay leaf, celery, thyme and seasoning. Cover and bake in a moderate oven 350°F for 2½ hours, basting occasionally. Test with a skewer. If the juices that run out are clear, the meat is cooked. Remove the meat from the oven, and cool.

Strain stock and, when cold, remove the fat. Boil the stock rapidly to reduce to a syrupy consistency. Cool slightly. Untie the meat, brush with glaze. Chill until ready to serve. Slice meat and garnish with sliced tomatoes, cucumbers and shredded lettuce or watercress. Serves 8-10.

Overleaf: A luncheon party for four set under the shade of a tree in the garden. Left to right: Italian refrigerator cake (p. 44), baked buttered mussels (p. 15), Greek country salad (p. 36) and roast stuffed pork (p. 20)

 COOK'S NOTES: Never discard left-over wine. You can use it for deglazing a roasting pan–red wine is especially good when making gravy. White wine is good for poaching fish. The bottles should be corked to keep wild yeasts at bay and they can be topped up with other wines, as long as the color is the same.

Vitello Tonnato

A perfect dish for a buffet party. I add a tablespoon of tomato paste to the tuna sauce to give a pretty color.

3   pound piece boneless veal fillet
2   anchovy fillets, cut into small pieces
1   tablespoon olive oil
1/3 cup dry vermouth
     Salt and pepper
     A bouquet garni
1   14-ounce can artichoke hearts
FOR THE SAUCE
6   ounces canned tuna
6   anchovy fillets
1   teaspoon capers
2   tablespoons lemon juice
1   tablespoon tomato paste, (optional)
     Salt and pepper
1/2 cup mayonnaise

Make some incisions in the surface of the meat with a sharp pointed knife and insert anchovy pieces. Roll up and tie neatly.

Heat the oil in a heavy casserole, preferably one into which the meat fits snugly, and brown the meat all over. Pour over the vermouth, season with salt and pepper then add the bouquet garni. Cover the casserole tightly and cook in a moderate oven (350°F) for 1-1¼ hours.

Remove from the oven and allow the veal to cool in the liquid, lift veal out and chill in the refrigerator to make the meat easier to carve.

To make the sauce, pound the tuna, anchovy fillets, capers, lemon juice and tomato paste (or process them in a blender) until smooth. Season with salt and pepper. Stir in the mayonnaise and then process in a blender or rub through a strainer.

Cut the veal into thick, even slices, spread each slice with the sauce and reshape the joint. Leave in the refrigerator until quite firm.

Serve surrounded by artichoke hearts which have been well-rinsed, drained and tossed in a flavored vinaigrette dressing. Alternatively, the veal may be cut into thin slices, arranged on a platter, then covered with the sauce and served with lemon wedges and a small dish of capers. Serves 8.

Endive & Ham Gratin

This newcomer to the vegetable scene, when combined with ham and cheese, makes an excellent first course for dinner or a good dish for a lunch party. You can prepare the dish in advance and reheat it in a hot oven.

8   endive heads
3   tablespoons lemon juice
1/2 cup chicken stock
1/2 teaspoon salt
     A pinch of superfine sugar
1   tablespoon butter
8   thin slices of ham
2   tablespoons grated cheese
FOR THE SAUCE
1/4 cup butter
2   tablespoons flour
2   cups warm milk
     Salt and pepper
2   tablespoons grated cheese

Remove outer leaves of the endive and cross the base with a knife. Wash under running water and drain. Place lemon juice, stock, salt, sugar and butter in a heavy skillet and bring to a boil. Put the endive in one layer on top, cover with a lid and simmer gently for 15 minutes, turn the vegetables around and cook for a further 5 minutes.

In the meantime, prepare the sauce by melting butter in a saucepan, adding the flour, and stirring briskly. Cook over a low heat for 1 minute, then slowly beat in warm milk. When the mixture is smooth, simmer for 15 minutes.

Drain the endive and wrap a slice of ham securely round each endive and place in a low-sided baking dish. Add liquid from the skillet to the sauce, stir, season with salt and pepper, add half the grated cheese. Pour sauce over endive. Scatter remaining 2 tablespoons of cheese on top and place under a broiler to brown when ready to serve. Serves 8.

Lasagne

Lasagne is an excellent dish for a buffet party. The meat sauce can be made in advance and the dish assembled on the day of the party, covered with foil and stored in the refrigerator until an hour before serving. Do allow plenty of time for the dish to heat up. You can bake it with the foil on top for the first 30 minutes, but it should be crisp and golden and piping hot when served. This is a very filling dish, so all you will need to complete the meal is a green salad and a light dessert.

FOR THE BOLOGNESE SAUCE
3/4   *pound ground beef*
1/4   *pound bacon*
1   *tablespoon butter or margarine*
1   *onion*
1   *carrot*
1   *celery stalk*
1   *garlic clove*
1/4   *pound chicken livers*
2/3   *cup tomato paste*
2/3   *cup dry wine*
1 1/4 cups water
1 chicken stock cube, salt, pepper and nutmeg
FOR THE BÉCHAMEL SAUCE
1/4   *cup butter or margarine*
3   *tablespoons flour*
2 1/2 cups milk
1   *bay leaf*
       Salt, pepper and nutmeg

1   *pound lasagne sheets*

COOK'S NOTES: Cayenne pepper is much stronger than black pepper. (In fact, it is so hot that it must be used in tiny pinches). But it is marvelous in sauces, smoked fish and cooked cheese dishes. Those who want a milder taste should use paprika, which is used in goulash and rice dishes and heightens the color of broiled or barbecued shellfish.

First make the Bolognese sauce. Chop bacon and sauté in butter. Chop onions, carrots and celery and crush the garlic. Add to the pan and stir well until lightly browned.

Cut the chicken livers in quarters and add to the pan with the ground beef and cook until well browned, stirring constantly. Add the remaining ingredients. Season to taste and simmer for 40 minutes.

Next make the béchamel sauce. Melt the butter in a pan, sprinkle in the flour and stir over low heat until thick and creamy–about 2 minutes. Heat the milk with the bay leaf and stir into flour and butter a little at a time. Bring to a boil and cook gently for 15 minutes, stirring occasionally. Remove the bay leaf and season.

To cook the pasta drop a sheet at a time into a large saucepan holding at least 2½ quarts of boiling salted water. Boil for 12 minutes, then drain in a strainer.

Grease the inside of a shallow ovenproof dish, about 10x15x2-inches. Spread a layer of the meat sauce on the base of the dish, top with a layer of the béchamel sauce, then lay lasagne sheets on top. Repeat layers, finishing with béchamel.

Sprinkle with grated cheese and bake in a preheated moderate oven (350°F) for 40-45 minutes or until heated through and brown on top. Cut into squares for serving. Serves 8-12.

To make this dish, you can choose fresh lasagne sheets. They are available at most supermarkets and Italian delicatessens. You do not need to boil them before layering in an ovenproof dish.

Baked Glazed Ham

14   *pound cured ham on the bone*
    10-pound boneless ham
FOR THE GLAZE
1 1/2 cups soft brown sugar
2   teaspoons dry mustard
1/2   cup clear honey
    Whole cloves
1/2   cup orange juice

Cut a scallop pattern around the thick end of the ham shank and ease skin away from the fat. Turn ham over and ease away remaining skin. Place the ham, fat side uppermost, on a rack in a roasting pan containing 1½-inches of water. Cover the pan with foil, making it as airtight as possible, and bake in a preheated moderately slow oven (325°F) for 1 hour. Remove from oven and pour off the liquid. Using a sharp knife, score fat with ¼-inch deep diagonal cuts, first one way, then the other, to form a diamond pattern.

Mix sugar, mustard and honey together and, using a brush, spread half the mixture over ham. Stud each diamond with a clove. Mix the remaining glaze with orange juice. Increase oven temperature to hot (400°F) and bake ham for a further 30-40 minutes, basting it every 10 minutes with remaining glaze. Serve hot or cold. Serves 20-25.

Chili con Carne

This is a wonderful dish for a teenage party. Notice that I have only used 1 teaspoon of chili powder. You may like to increase the amount but don't make it too hot. If you are busy, you can use canned red kidney beans.

1   pound red kidney beans
1/2   teaspoon ground cumin
1   garlic clove, crushed
    A few stalks of parsley
1   onion, stuck with a few whole cloves
2   bay leaves
2   teaspoons salt
2 1/2 pounds ground beef
2   onions, finely chopped
2   garlic cloves, crushed
4   tablespoons olive oil
1   cup beef stock
    or water and bouilion cubes
1   14-ounce can tomato purée
2   tablespoons tomato paste
    Salt
1   teaspoon chili powder
2   teaspoons dried oregano leaves
    or 1 sprig fresh oregano
1   teaspoon cumin

Soak the beans, overnight. Next day, drain and place in a large saucepan. Add 6 cups water, bring to a boil and boil rapidly for 10 minutes. Add the cumin, garlic, parsley, onion, bay leaves and salt. Cover and simmer gently for 1½ hours. Remove the onions, bay leaves and parsley stalks, drain the beans and set aside.

Heat oil in a pan and add chopped onions, gently cooking them until soft. Add the garlic and fry gently for 1 minute. Remove to a dish and keep warm. Add more oil to the pan if necessary, and brown the meat over a high heat, stirring constantly.

When meat is brown, add the onions and garlic, stir in the stock, tomato purée, tomato paste, salt, chili powder, oregano and cumin.

Chili con carne is a homely dish that continues to be a firm favorite with my family.

Cover the pan and simmer for 30 minutes. Add the drained beans and simmer for a further 30 minutes until they are tender. Adjust seasoning before serving. Serves 8-10.

COOK'S NOTES: To carve a ham, first remove a slice from underneath, to allow the ham to sit flat. With a sharp knife, make a vertical cut approximately 4-inches from the knuckle. Make a second cut at an angle to the first and remove the wedge formed. Cut several thin slices right down to the bone, parallel to the second cut. Carve along the bone and remove slices.

CHICKEN

Arroz con Pollo

You can substitute thighs and legs for the whole chicken but if possible always use saffron threads as they give the right flavor. Serve with either rice or pasta followed by a green salad.

2	2½-pound chickens, each cut into 6 pieces
2	teaspoons dried oregano
1/2	teaspoon pepper
	Salt
1/2	cup salad oil
2	cups onion finely chopped
1	garlic clove, crushed
1	medium sized green sweet pepper
1	bay leaf
1/4	teaspoon paprika
1	teaspoon saffron threads
2	cups long grain rice
1	14-ounce can tomatoes
2	cups chicken stock
1/2	pound frozen green peas
1	red sweet pepper

Wash the chicken pieces and dry well. Combine oregano, pepper and 2 teaspoons salt. Sprinkle the mixture all over the chicken. Rub in well. leave for 10 minutes.

In a large heavy casserole, heat the oil over medium heat. Brown the chicken a third at a time until golden-brown all over. Remove the chicken and keep warm.

Cut green pepper into lengthwise strips, ½-inch wide. To the drippings in casserole, add the onion, garlic, green sweet pepper, bay leaf and paprika, and sauté, stirring, over medium heat until the onion is tender.

Using the back of a spoon, crush the saffron threads on a small piece of foil. Add rice with 2 teaspoons salt to the casserole. Cook, stirring, until rice is lightly browned, about 10 minutes. Add the undrained tomatoes and chicken stock. Arrange chicken over the rice mixture. Bring to a boil. Bake, covered, in a preheated moderate oven (350°F) for 1 hour.

Remove from the oven and add ½ cup water. Sprinkle peas over the top. Cut red pepper into ½-inch strips and arrange attractively over the top. Bake, covered for a further 20 minutes or until chicken is tender, peas are cooked and rice has absorbed all the liquid. Remove from oven and leave to stand, covered, for 10 minutes. Serve from the casserole. Serves 8.

Oven-Fried Lemon Chicken

2	2½-pound chickens
1	cup flour
2	teaspoons salt
1/2	teaspoon pepper
1	tablespoon paprika
3/4	cup butter or margarine
FOR THE SAUCE	
1	tablespoon soy sauce
1	teaspoon pepper
1/2	cup oil
1/2	cup lemon juice
1	tablespoon grated lemon rind
2	garlic cloves, crushed

Oven-fried lemon chicken is a succulent dish, perfect for entertaining. It can be made well in advance and just put in the oven when needed, leaving you plenty of time to talk to the guests.

Combine all the sauce ingredients, mix well and refrigerate for 1 hour.

Combine the flour, salt, pepper and paprika. Cut the chicken into serving sized pieces and toss in seasoned flour. Grease a large ovenproof dish. Arrange chicken pieces skin-side down in single layer. Melt butter, spoon over chicken, bake uncovered in a preheated hot oven (400°F) for 30 minutes. Then turn chicken, spoon over lemon sauce and cook for a further 30 minutes or until tender, basting occasionally. Serves 8-12.

COOK'S NOTES: When decorating with sliced eggs, it is important that the yolk is in the middle of the slice. This can be achieved by moving the eggs around in the pan while they are cooking. When cooked, place eggs in a bowl of cold running water to prevent over cooking. They are easy to peel if lightly tapped to break the seal between the shell and the egg.

Not only is Circassian chicken a delicious treat, it is actually good for you.

Coq au Vin

This is the classic French recipe and is really worth the effort for a special dinner party.

1	*3-pound chicken*
2	*cups red wine*
2	*bay leaves*
	A sprig of thyme
1	*garlic clove*
	Chicken stock
	Salt and pepper
2	*tablespoons oil*
2	*tablespoons butter*
1/4	*pound of ham shoulder, diced*
12	*small onions*
1/2	*pound mushrooms*
1/4	*cup brandy*
	A bouquet garni
1	*garlic clove*
2	*tablespoons butter*
2	*teaspoons flour*

Place the red wine in a saucepan with the bay

leaves, thyme, garlic clove and chicken stock. Bring to a boil and reduce by half. Set aside.

Divide chicken into serving sized pieces (or chicken pieces may be used). Wipe dry with paper towel and season.

Heat oil in a heavy based skillet with a lid. Add the butter and, when it begins to froth, add the chicken pieces. Sauté a few pieces at a time until golden-brown. Remove and set aside.

Add the ham to the pan. When the fat starts to run, add the onions and sauté until starting to color. Trim mushrooms and wipe clean. Add to the onions in the pan and sauté quickly. Return chicken pieces to the pan. Heat the brandy in a ladle or small saucepan, ignite and pour while flaming into the skillet.

Pour the reduced wine mixture over the chicken. Add bouquet garni and garlic, crushed with a little salt. Bring to a boil, cover and simmer gently for 30-35 minutes or until the chicken is tender. Remove the bouquet garni.

Transfer chicken into a heated serving dish, leaving pan juices and keep warm. Combine the butter and flour to a paste and drop small pieces into the pan juices. Simmer over a low heat, whisking continuously, until the sauce begins to thicken. Bring to a boil and cook for 2 minutes.

Spoon the sauce over the chicken. Garnish with croûtes of fried bread dipped in a little chopped parsley. Serves 6.

COOKS NOTES: To make croûtes, remove crusts from three thick slices of stale bread. Cut each slice into four triangles and fry in 1-inch of hot oil. When golden, remove, sprinkle with salt and keep warm in the oven.

Circassian Chicken

A famous Turkish cold chicken specialty which would rate a place of honor at any buffet. The sauce is very wholesome and easy to make if you have a blender or food processor.

4	pounds chicken pieces
1	onion
1	carrot
	A few sprigs of parsley
1	teaspoon salt
1/2	teaspoon pepper
FOR THE SAUCE	
2	cups walnut halves
3	slices white bread
1	cup chicken stock
1-2	tablespoons walnut oil
1	tablespoon paprika

Place chicken, onion, carrot, parsley, salt and pepper in a pan and cover with water. Simmer very gently for about 1 hour, or until the chicken is tender, but not falling apart. Leave to stand, covered, until cool.

Remove the skin and bones from the chicken and cut pieces into strips and set aside in refrigerator while preparing the sauce. Place the walnuts and 1 slice of bread in a food processor and blend until fairly smooth. Break the remaining bread into cubes and drop into the machine while it is still running. Then slowly add chicken stock through the feed tube, just as if you were making mayonnaise. When a smooth consistency has been obtained, season with salt and pepper if necessary. Mix half the walnut paste with the chicken and place in serving dish. Cover with remaining paste. Just before serving, combine oil and paprika and dribble over the surface. This dish is always served chilled. Serves 8.

Split the chicken breasts in half and flatten lightly. Place in shallow saucepan with the remaining ingredients. Add almost sufficient water to cover chicken and cook, covered, over medium heat for about 10 minutes, or until the chicken is just cooked. Remove from heat and allow to cool.

Place egg, egg yolks and mustard in a food processor and work for 30 seconds, then add oil in a slow, steady stream through the feed tube until a thick mayonnaise is formed. Add half the lemon juice, then the tuna fish after removing any bones.

Finally, add the anchovy fillets and about 2 teaspoons of tomato paste–just enough to give a pretty pink color to the sauce. If the sauce is too thick, add the remaining lemon juice and some cold poaching liquid. Season to taste, remembering the anchovies are very salty.

Remove the chicken breasts from the cold poaching liquid and slice into bite-sized pieces. Pack into a plastic container and cover with most of the sauce chill overnight. To serve, arrange on a flat serving dish, cover with the remaining sauce and garnish with watercress, lemon wedges and salted capers. Serves 25-30.

Chicken Tonnato

This is a lovely dish for a wedding reception. It is a variation of *Veal Tonnato* and so easy to make if you are entertaining a large party.

10	chicken breasts, skinned and boneless
1	cup white wine
2	lemon slices
1	celery stalk, sliced
1	bay leaf
	A few black peppercorns
1	teaspoon salt

FOR THE SAUCE
1	egg
2	egg yolks
1	teaspoon Dijon mustard
2	cups olive oil
	Juice of 1 lemon
1	cup canned tuna fish
6	anchovy fillets
	Tomato paste
	Salt and pepper

FOR THE GARNISH
	Sprigs of watercress
	Lemon wedges
	Salted capers

 COOK'S NOTES: Egg shells are very porous so be careful either to store eggs in a refrigerator or a cool place and never near any strong smell, whether pleasant or unpleasant.

 COOK'S NOTES: Dry a few pieces of orange, lemon or mandarin peel in a moderate oven while cooking something else. They add a delicious aroma to casseroles, especially beef or oxtail. Store the dried peel in an airtight jar and use as you would a bay leaf. Dried orange peel is particularly nice in compote of fruit.

SALADS

Celeriac Salad

Celeriac is usually available in the winter months and makes the most delicious salads. Do take care, however, to keep it in cold water and add the dressing just before serving.

1/2	pound celeriac peeled
2	tablespoons salad oil
1	tablespoon vinegar
1/2	teaspoon French mustard
	Salt and pepper
1	green shallot, finely chopped
1	tablespoon chopped parsley

Cut the celeriac into thin, matchstick strips. Cover with cold water, adding a slice of lemon and a cube of ice. Combine the oil, vinegar, mustard, salt and pepper. Beat well, add the shallot and parsley. Drain the celeriac well and toss in the dressing. Serve surrounded by sliced tomato. Serves 6.

Avocado Salad

This valuable fruit harbors no less than eleven vitamins and makes the most delicious salads. This salad is best served soon after preparation and is very popular with people who don't like salad oil.

2	ripe avocados
2	tomatoes, finely chopped
1	small onion, finely chopped
1	teaspoon paprika
1	teaspoon salt
1/2	teaspoon pepper
	Juice of 1 lemon
1	romaine lettuce, thoroughly washed
1	tablespoon chopped parsley

Halve avocados, peel and cut into small pieces. In a deep bowl, mash the avocados, tomatoes and onion with the back of a large spoon. Add paprika, salt and pepper, pour on the lemon juice and stir well. Line the bottom and sides of a salad bowl or a large plate with the romaine lettuce leaves. Add avocado salad to the center of the bowl and garnish with the chopped parsley. Chill in the refrigerator for 30 minutes and serve. Serves 6-8.

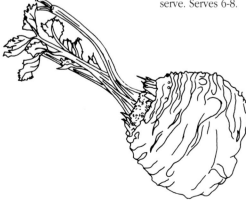

Seafood Salad

For friends who do not eat red meat, I usually try to have a fish salad on the buffet table. You can choose any fish that is free from bones.

1 kg	(2 lb) white fish, cooked
1 kg	(2 lb) new potatoes, boiled
	Salt and pepper
1	small cucumber, peeled and diced
10	radishes, sliced
2	teaspoons capers
2	red apples, diced
4	hard-boiled eggs, chopped
	Mayonnaise
	Lettuce
	Tomatoes
	Lemon

Take fish and cut the potatoes into small dice. Toss together with salt and pepper, cucumber, radishes, capers, apple and eggs. Add enough mayonnaise to bind. Spoon into a plain mold and leave until ready to serve.

Turn out onto a bed of lettuce and garnish with tomato slices and lemon wedges. Serves 8.

Greek Country Salad

1	lettuce
	A bunch of radishes
1	cucumber
4	tomatoes
1/2	cup black olives
1/2	pound fetta cheese
FOR THE DRESSING	
5	tablespoons olive oil
1 1/2	tablespoon vinegar
2	garlic cloves, crushed
2	tablespoons chopped mint
	Salt and pepper

Mushrooms à la Grecque

This recipe can be varied according to the vegetables available. Zucchinis are very good cooked this way. Top and tail the vegetables and cut into bite-sized pieces.

1	pound button mushrooms
1	tablespoon fresh tarragon
	or 1 teaspoon dried tarragon
1	tablespoon lemon juice
1	garlic clove
1	tablespoon finely chopped parsley
1	tomato, peeled, seeded and chopped
	A pinch of thyme
	Salt and pepper
1	bay leaf
1/4	cup olive oil
1	cup water

Carefully wipe the mushrooms, trim stems, and slice lengthwise. Place with remaining ingredients in a heavy saucepan. Cover and bring to a boil. Reduce the heat and cook gently until mushrooms are tender but firm, 8-10 minutes. Leave to cool, then chill. Serve with crusty rolls. Serves 6-8.

Opposite: Greek country salad is perfect for an outdoor summer lunch party. People have been enjoying this type of salad for hundreds of years.

Wash the lettuce and crisp in the refrigerator. Trim radishes, cut cucumber in thick slices and tomatoes in wedges. Tear lettuce into bite-sized pieces and place in bowl with prepared vegetables, black olives and fetta cheese cut into 1-inch cubes.

Combine the dressing ingredients, shake well and pour over the salad. Toss and serve immediately. Serves 8.

Scandinavian Yogurt Salad

This is a nice way of serving cucumber for those who don't like oil.

1	cucumber
1	teaspoon salt
1	tablespoon finely chopped onion
1	tablespoon chopped dill pickles
1/2	cup yogurt
	Salt and pepper
2	teaspoons chopped chives or dill.

COOK'S NOTES: It is advisable to snip chives finely just before you serve, as their flavor is best when freshly prepared. This is usually done with scissors directly over a bowl of green salad or scrambled eggs.

Peel cucumber and slice finely. Sprinkle with salt, allow to stand for 30 minutes, then drain. Combine onion, dill pickles and yogurt. Add to the drained cucumber.

Season to taste and garnish with chives or dill. Serves 6.

Spinach Salad with Yogurt Dressing

This is a good salad to serve at a party as it is popular with guests who are on a low-fat diet. Choose very tender, young spinach leaves or if these are not available, corn salad lettuce, a mixture of several kinds of salad greens usually obtainable in ready-to-use packages from supermarkets.

1/2	pound young spinach
3	ounces ricotta cheese
2	tablespoons yogurt
1	tablespoon wine vinegar
2	tablespoons chopped chives
1	tablespoon chopped parsley
	Salt and pepper

Remove any stalks from the spinach, wash the leaves and gently pat dry with paper towels. Roll up leaves like a cigar and slice into 1-inch strips. In a large mixing bowl beat the cheese and yogurt until smooth, add the vinegar, chopped chives and parsley then season with salt and pepper. If the dressing is too thick, add a little more yogurt.

When ready to serve, add the spinach to the dressing and toss and roll the salad. Turn into a salad bowl and decorate with the flowers of chives or marigold petals. Serves 6.

I decorated the spinach salad with yogurt dressing and rosebuds to make it look extra special.

Curried Chicken & Mango Salad

This is an excellent salad for a party and can be made ahead. This quantity will serve 6 but it is quite easy to double or treble the recipe.

2	chicken breasts, cut in halves
1	tablespoon lemon juice
2	mangoes, peeled and sliced
1	cup celery chopped
1/4	cup natural yogurt
1/4	cup mayonnaise
1 1/2	teaspoons curry powder
1/2	teaspoon ground cumin
3/4	cup roasted cashew nuts, chopped
2	tablespoons chopped cilantro leaves
	Mixed salad greens, washed and crisp

Poach chicken breasts in salted water to cover for about 15 minutes, and allow to cool in a pan of stock. Remove skin and bones and cut chicken into bite-sized pieces. Combine the chicken, lemon juice, mangoes, celery and shallots. In a small bowl whisk together the yogurt, mayonnaise, curry powder and cumin. Add the dressing to the chicken mixture with salt and pepper to taste. Cover and chill for several hours.

Just before serving, stir in the cashews and cilantro. Serve on crisp salad greens. Serves 6.

COOK'S NOTES: *Always add a tablespoon of cold water to the egg you are using for egg and bread crumbs. Lightly beat the egg and water, dip the food in this mixture, then in the bread crumbs. Press lightly with a palette knife or your hand and leave to stand for an hour or so. This makes for maximum adhesion.*

DESSERTS

Sweet Sherry Trifle

It is very easy to double this recipe. But if you do so you will need two large glass dishes.

1	jelly roll, cut into 1-inch slices
2	teaspoons gelatin
1/4	cup hot water
3/4	cup sweet sherry
3	eggs, separated
5	tablespoons superfine sugar
2	tablespoons lemon juice
3/4	cup heavy cream
	Extra heavy cream for decorating

Brush a glass dish with a little sherry. Line the dish with jelly roll slices. Dissolve gelatin in hot water, then add the sherry. Cool, then chill for 30 minutes or until mixture thickens.

Meanwhile, beat the egg yolks until frothy, add 2 tablespoons sugar gradually and beat until yolks are thick and lemony colored. Whip egg whites until frothy. Add remaining sugar gradually, beating constantly. Add the lemon juice and beat until the mixture is stiff but not dry.

Add slightly thickened sherry and gelatin mixture into egg yolks and combine well. Whip the cream and lightly fold in. Lastly, fold in egg whites gently but thoroughly. Pour into lined glass dish. Chill until firm. Serve decorated with extra whipped cream. Serves 8.

Brandy Snaps

An old-fashioned dessert which can be made a few days in advance of your party and 'filled' shortly before your guests arrive.

1/4   cup butter
1/3   cup soft light brown sugar
1/3   cup light corn syrup
1   teaspoon ground ginger
1/2   cup flour, sifted
2   teaspoons each lemon juice and rind
      Whipped cream to fill, (optional)

Lightly grease two baking sheets. Gently warm the butter, sugar, syrup and ginger in a heavy-based saucepan until the butter has melted and you have a syrupy liquid. Add the sifted flour and lemon.

Take generous teaspoonfuls of the mixture and tap them out, five round dollops to each baking sheet, spaced well apart. Bake for 15 minutes in a preheated hot oven (425°F). They will spread into malleable, lacy discs.

Before they cool to hardness, lift each in turn with a palette knife or spatula and roll it neatly around the handle of a greased wooden spoon. Allow curls to stand on a wire rack.

They are lovely on their own, or meltingly delicious if filled at each end with whipped cream containing tiny fragments of preserved ginger and a spoonful of the ginger syrup.

They store well in an airtight tin for several days. Once filled, chill, and make sure they are eaten within a few hours.

Sweet Sherry Trifle

It is very easy to double this recipe. But if you do so you will need two large glass dishes.

1 jam sponge roll, cut into 2.5cm (1 in.) slices
2   teaspoons gelatin
60 g (2 oz) water
185 ml   (6 fl oz) sweet sherry
3   eggs, separated
5   tablespoons superfine sugar
2   tablespoons lemon juice
155ml (1/4 pint) whipping cream
      Extra whipping cream for decorating

Brush a glass dish with a little sherry. Line the dish with jam sponge slices. Dissolve gelatin in hot water and then add the sherry. Cool, then chill for 30 minutes or until mixture begins to thicken.

Meanwhile, beat the egg yolks until frothy, add 2 tablespoons superfine sugar gradually and beat until yolks are thick and lemony colored. Whip egg whites until frothy. Add remaining sugar gradually, beating constantly. Add the lemon juice and beat until the mixture is stiff but not dry.

Add slightly thickened sherry and gelatin mixture into egg yolks and combine well. Whip the cream and lightly fold in. Lastly, fold in egg whites gently but thoroughly.

Pour into lined glass dish. Chill until firm. Serve decorated with extra whipped cream. Serves 8.

Compote of Fruit

2   pounds fruit of your choice
1/2   cup granulated sugar
1 1/4 cups water
      A few drops of vanilla essence

Make sweet sherry trifle with chocolate sponge roll for a change. It is easy to make and looks so special.

Prepare the fruit. Place the sugar and water in a saucepan and stir over low heat until sugar has dissolved. Bring to a boil and simmer for 2 minutes, then lower heat and add fruit. Poach fruit gently until just cooked (do not allow fruit to become too soft). Remove to a dish with a slotted spoon, and reduce the syrup a little by boiling rapidly. Add the vanilla. Pour syrup over the fruit. Allow to cool, then chill.

Grand Marnier Soufflé

We all want to make a dramatic soufflé for some special dinner and here is a sensational recipe given to me by the chef Jean Delaunay.

2	tablespoons superfine sugar for dusting
1/4	cup butter
2	tablespoons flour
2	teaspoons cornstarch
1 1/4	cup milk, warmed
2	tablespoons superfine sugar
	Grated zest of 1 orange
3	tablespoons Grand Marnier
4	egg yolks
5	egg whites
1	tablespoon superfine sugar

Grease a large soufflé dish and tie around it a collar of doubled, greased waxed paper to come 1½-inches above the dish edge. Dust inside the dish with superfine sugar, turn it upside down and tap the base to remove excess sugar. Preheat oven to hot (400°F) and place a baking sheet on the center shelf.

Melt the butter in a saucepan over low heat, add flour and cornstarch then stir for 1 minute. Remove from heat, cool a little, then add warm milk. Stir until smoothly blended, then return to heat and stir until boiling. Boil for 30 seconds, remove from heat and stir in sugar. Stir in zest, Grand Marnier and egg yolks, one at a time. Turn the mixture into a large bowl.

Whisk egg whites until they hold soft peaks. Stir a large spoonful of whites into the egg yolk mixture, then scoop the remaining whites on top. Fold in with a large metal spoon or rubber spatula, using a down, up and over cutting motion and turning the bowl a little each time.

Turn the mixture into the prepared soufflé dish and place it on the heated baking sheet. Immediately turn the oven down to moderately hot (375°F) and bake for 20 minutes without opening the oven door. Then open the door gently, sprinkle superfine sugar on top of the soufflé and bake for 10-15 minutes longer, until soufflé is well risen and brown.

Place the dish on a heated serving platter, remove the paper collar and take immediately to the table. To serve, spread the top apart with a warmed serving spoon and fork then serve some of the firm outside and creamy center with each portion. Serves 6.

Lemon Soufflé

You can substitute limes for lemons, but whatever fruit you use, this is an ever-popular party dessert.

1/2	cup hot water
4	teaspoons gelatin
4	eggs, separated
1	cup superfine sugar
4	tablespoons lemon juice
1	tablespoon grated lemon peel
1 1/4	cups heavy cream
	Thin lemon slices
1	cup heavy cream to decorate

Cut a band of waxed paper or foil long enough to wrap around the outside of a large soufflé dish. Fold in half, then wrap around the dish to make a collar that stands 2-inches above the dish edge. Secure with an elastic band, adhesive tape and, if necessary, use a paper clip to keep edges together.

Place hot water in a cup, add gelatin, and stir briskly until dissolved. Set aside. Whisk the egg yolks until thick, then gradually beat in sugar. When the mixture is thick and white, add the lemon juice and peel, beat a further minute, then beat in dissolved gelatin and keep beating until mixture is thick and fluffy.

Beat egg whites until stiff but not dry and fold into the egg yolk mixture gently but thoroughly. Whip the cream until it holds soft peaks (do not over beat), and fold gently into the egg mixture. Pour into prepared soufflé dish and chill overnight, or for at least 4 hours.

To serve, remove the band of paper from thedish and decorate soufflé with lemon slices and stiffly whipped cream. Serves 8.

Rice Tyrolhof with Apricot Sauce

You can use any fruit except pineapple for this creamy pudding. The gelatin will not set when in contact with raw pineapple.

FOR THE RICE
1   cup short-grain rice
2 1/2 cups milk
2   eggs, separated
2   tablespoons superfine sugar
1   orange
2   teaspoons gelatin
1   dessert apple, diced
1   cup strawberries or grapes sliced
1   tablespoon finely chopped, candied peel

Rice Tyrolhof is one of the most attractive sweet rice dishes I have ever tasted.

FOR THE APRICOT SAUCE
1/2   cup apricot jam
1   tablespoon lemon juice
2   teaspoons lemon peel
3   tablespoons hot water

Combine all the sauce ingredients and chill. Simmer rice with milk until soft and creamy, 25-30 minutes. Remove from heat. Beat egg yolk with sugar and stir into the rice. Add 2 teaspoons grated orange peel and candied peel.

Dissolve gelatin in the orange juice over hot water and add to the rice with fruit. When cool, add beaten egg white and pour into a serving dish. Chill. Serve with apricot sauce. Serves 6.

Italian Refrigerator Cake

A rich, luscious cake is always a favorite and this is one of the most delicious cakes imaginable. The sponge layers are very light and delicate and use only 2 eggs, but if you are very busy, you can use a bought sponge cake.

1   cup flour
3/4   teaspoon baking powder
1/4   teaspoon salt
2   egg yolks
1/2   cup cold water
1   cup superfine sugar
1   teaspoon vanilla extract
1/2   teaspoon lemon extract
2   egg whites
FOR THE FROSTING
1/3   cup chocolate chips
3/4   cup superfine sugar
1   pound ricotta cheese
1/2   teaspoon ground cloves
2   tablespoons grated lemon peel
2   tablespoons grated orange peel
2   tablespoons sweet vermouth

Sift the flour, baking powder and salt together. Beat the egg yolks and water until fluffy and treble in volume. Add the sugar gradually and continue beating until light and thick.

Stir in the vanilla and lemon extract, then add the flour mixture all at once, folding it in with a rubber spatula or a metal spoon.

Whisk the egg whites until stiff peaks form, and fold into the mixture. Place in two greased and lined 8-inch sandwich tins and bake in a preheated moderate oven (350°F) for 20-25 minutes.

Invert the pans on wire racks and leave until they are cold. Remove the pans and lining paper.

Melt the chocolate chips in a bowl over hot water. Stir in the sugar and remaining ingredients, except vermouth, and mix well. Chill in the refrigerator for 30 minutes before using. Put one cake layer onto a serving plate. Sprinkle with half the vermouth and spread with less than half the filling. Top with a second layer and sprinkle with the remaining vermouth and then spread the frosting over the top and sides of cake using a palette knife.

Chill for about 4 hours before serving. You can decorate the cake with whipped cream just before serving or serve with a bowl of whipped cream handed round separately. Serves 8.

Above: Italian refrigerator cake is very fast to make if you buy the sponges. Ricotta cheese makes excellent desserts.

Grease two baking sheets and line them with greased and floured waxed paper. Have egg whites ready at room temperature.

Beat the egg whites until foamy, add the baking powder and beat until whites hold firm peaks. Add 2 tablespoons of sugar, beating for 3 minutes more or until stiff. Sprinkle remaining sugar over and fold in with a metal spoon.

Using a plain ½-inch piping tip, pipe small, high spirals of meringue, slightly apart, on the prepared baking sheets. (Or you may shape meringues with two tablespoons dipped in hot water: scoop up meringue with one spoon and use the other to shape the top and push it onto the baking sheet.) Bake in a preheated very slow oven (200°F) for 1½ hours or until they are completely dry. If meringues are coloring too much, open oven door slightly.

Lift meringues from sheets and cool on a wire rack. The meringues may be stored in an airtight container for several weeks, or frozen for longer periods.

To make the sauce, wash fruit. Bring water and sugar to a boil, add fruit and heat gently. Rub through a strainer or purée in a food processor. Add Grand Marnier or orange peel. Cover and store in refrigerator until required.

The cream filling may be made several hours ahead–the egg white will keep it firm. Whip the cream, egg white, confectioners' sugar and vanilla together until stiff. Cover and refrigerate.

About an hour before you want to serve, sandwich the meringues together in pairs with a good spoonful of the filling, pile them up on a serving dish and serve with a bowl of fruit sauce. Makes 30.

Meringues with Fruit Sauce

FOR THE MERINGUES
4   egg whites
     A good pinch of tartrate baking powder
1   cup superfine sugar
FOR THE FRUIT SAUCE
1/2   pound raspberries or strawberries
1   cup water
1/4   cup superfine sugar
2   tablespoons Grand Marnier,
     other orange liqueur or brandy,
     or 1 teaspoon grated orange peel
FOR THE CREAM FILLING
1   cup heavy cream, chilled
1   egg white
2   teaspoons confectioners' sugar
1/2   teaspoon vanilla extract

 COOK'S NOTES: Always choose a metal spoon in preference to a wooden spoon when folding in egg white. The job is easier if you first mix in a tablespoon of the beaten egg white before folding in the remainder.

Champagne Sorbet

For a special birthday party, serve this delicious dessert in chilled champagne glasses and top with champagne at the table.

1 1/2   cups water
1   cup granulated sugar
        Grated peel of 2 lemons
        Juice of 2 lemons
1 1/4   cups heavy cream
1 1/4   cups unflavored yogurt
1/4   bottle sweet champagne
1   egg white

Place the water, sugar with the lemon peel in a saucepan and simmer for 10 minutes. Cool and combine with the lemon juice. Lightly whip the cream, fold in yogurt and strain in cooled lemon juice and syrup.

Pour into a container and freeze until mushy. Remove from the freezer, beat well and then add the champagne. Freeze again to the mushy stage. Beat again and fold in the stiffly beaten egg white. Freeze until firm and serve with a sponge fingers or wafers. Serves 8.

You can use any extra champagne to top up the champagne sorbet, or drink it separately. Whichever way, it is bound to be a success.

Strawberry Palmiers

With frozen puff pastry readily available, these delectable cakes are so easy to make. Just remember to insure that the pastries are quite cold before filling with cream.

1/2   pound package frozen puff pastry, thawed
1/3   cup superfine sugar
1/4   cup strawberry jam
3/4   cup heavy cream, whipped
3/4   cup strawberries, halved
      Confectioners' sugar for dredging

Roll out the pastry on a well sugared surface to a rectangle about 12x10-inches. Sprinkle with the sugar and press it in with a rolling pin. Take the shorter edges of the pastry and roll them up to meet in the center. Moisten with water and press together to join the two rolls. Cut into ½-inch slices and place well apart, cut-side down, on a dampened baking sheet, flattening them slightly.

Bake in a preheated hot oven (425°F) for 12-15 minutes. Turn the palmiers over when they begin to brown, so that both sides caramelise. Transfer to a wire rack to cool. Spread half the palmiers with jam. Spoon the cream into a piping bag fitted with a ½-inch fluted tip and pipe swirls of cream onto jam. Arrange a few strawberries on the cream and top with remaining palmiers. Press down and sprinkle with confectioners' sugar. Makes 6.

COOK'S NOTES: A cube of sugar in a cookie tin helps to absorb moisture and to keep the cookies fresh and crisp.

COOK'S NOTES: Chocolate should not be stored in a refrigerator as it will sweat when it returns to room temperature, and the moisture will discolor the chocolate, leaving white spots when it dries. A cool, dry, dark place is best.

INDEX

Page numbers in **bold** type indicate illustrations.